The Fire
is
Breathing On Me

Poems by
Mat Gould

Printed in the United States of America

First printing 2010
Second printing 2013

ISBN 978-0-9855291-2-3

Dog On A Chain Press
c/o Beasley Barrenton
503 Silverleaf Rd.
Zionville, NC 28698

For ordering information or all other inquiry
dogonachainpress@yahoo.com

for contributor credits/permission see back page(s)

"You are like a swamp animal during an eclipse." <u>James Tate</u>

the rule of a ruined kingdom-

-

the thriving crusade

here is an afternoon
of course
the barrage is everywhere
the weather
the bill collectors
the patrons
the drones
the la de da

it is damn near a debacle of faith
severing every head
hanging them as a carousel along the street
keeping them lit
so they can be followed out of town
and anyone incoming
may heed the warning
or sense the enchantment-

the gist of being alive

in the morning we join the doves
and all that was
debris
nothing but dust that doan douse the fire

poetry had been walking in the dark
until I put my tongue back in my mouth
it had been drinking the few beers that were left
from other days and nights
it was lonely and seductive
thinking about a midnight romance
in a small-scale town not quite a city
but still full of brick

feeding the old to the young at such an hour
has become too much for itself
a bit of ash in what has spilled
a feint break in the hue
a
dream
of
flight
a quintessence at the edge

under these bones we come out of our skin
not so much gasping as grasping for the split-

**make a move or feel the urgent hand of sacrifice slap you like
a silly bastard**

I take back what I said about myself
then again
oh, then again

what the fuck is that
shit, I would have kept my face planted in the stink of drool on the
pillow
for no reason what so ever
but there were birds
and traffic
and I was still in need of commotions punch
I sat up
I had done this before
seemingly everyday for quite awhile
it is going to continue this way
I will not deem this a problem

acceptance has such a pretty face
tolerance takes the ugly form of anything else
so on to the highlights
I crack my neck, twist my back to no adieu but the stiff bolts
of the sore rump I am used to
stand up
now standing here
foot to the grid
that's all I needed
yes
that certainly was-

the 10 count

doan be so sure of yourself
bullshit
be as sure as it gets
certain as sure as the shit itself
if not more
careful what you ask for
shit again
I asked for all of this
practically pleaded for the rite
the complete stampede
hoof to mouth
so I gotsta do something with it

to impress the sun
a champ has to sweat
a champ has to induce frenzy
a champ has to pay
with the pain that was promised
once
in a younger day
a champ has to keep you on your knees
content
with
mercy-

charcoal drawings of a century known for the demise of sense

anything for good measure
step back a few feet
pucker up
spit toward the breeze
walk it off
poke at the hive with a flimsy stick
find smoke
from a burning wick of tobacco and paper
wilderness messed with oil
a pheromone incense at the back of your neck
blood from the nose of the stumbling giant
smudged on my face by the stone hands of liberty

every tongue licking the gibberish
from the metal slate
put the grub
back
on the dirty plate
swathe the imbecile with gristle and fat
so that he may be hung out back to dry with the feed-

stick and jab...getting back to Barrenton

I needed a break from clarity
not to mention
the wounded coyote
that is this older fella held up just over from me
singing
"it makes me wonder..."
me too,
the product of thought gets carried away
a bit inane
I took up a conversation with the humidity
a bit agitated
we came to an agreement
that we doan care to care much for each other
yet we could admire the staunch and stifle
and my dependency upon breath

perhaps jes leaving it at that
some of us go on
and some of us wage malevolence
waiting for the fitful torrent to relent-

riding at the helm of a manual 442

fuck if I wouldn't almost pray for rain right now
dancin' won't do nah good
as harmless as it may seem
the dust is laughter's intrigue

one of the cats is jumping at the door
I have opened up the typewriter
I thought for sure The Sterling was going to turn away
or worse, spew drivel and curse at me
I had kept the lid shut all winter long
now looking under the hood
I got a hunch I need it more than ever
jes to keep from the gallows

the bridge is up
the ship is underneath
I am throwing small stones at its mast
there is no stalemate
each of us has staved off the rage
with every touch my throat gets tighter
fingers in the curve slide back out
strip off the skirt
and entreat the downpour-

whatever the usual may be

barge in on the sunset, ask for a drink
take what you can get
the fix is in
sleep on the couch
counter-act the circumstance

I am not fully aware as to what that means
or if there is a risk involved with such

use up the profanity dictionary
add some words to it
come up for air
and then get back in between those thighs
give it all a real spritz shine

smell everything in the morning
-seems like somebody used cleaning products outside-

but they didn't get the floor that's for sure
with consecutive steps I stepped on sticky spots
trying to dry up
jes passed the stove

check your face for ramifications of days gone by
bare thee chest to the open mouths of the wolves den
watch a few innings, if all goes well
feel free to label it "according to plan"
nobody will ever know you clocked out early
without actually clocking out
and nobody will ever know you lucked out
or so you think-

starlings

a croak from the backyard wire
another from the gutter
I am usually in and out of one or the other
a sudden change in the weather
it gets better
I guess
but I doan know how to tell the difference
because the starlings never change their song-

an astronomical simplicity in the hands of conquerors

the barbarians have calmed
changed face
they have given the world to their children
who play with it like medieval ingrates
as if it is a flattening beach ball
pushing it around
kicking it harder than necessary
and never blowing it back up to toss in a circle of cheer
letting it deflate and lie there in muck
they have no idea it is begging to bounce
hand
upon
hand
thrusting and bumping
back amongst the planets
steadying its orbit
a vision that takes what is known as millions of years to create-

the skull and crossbones(this is a lonely place without you and me)

the sea is not flat
it curls into itself
bends at the waist
of
nights
and
days

the sea is not selfish
it sends pieces of the shore
to other shores
it sinks the occasional ship
yet is willing to let any ghost go

the sea is a lover
and that is hard to do-

the sudden abundance of thrones

it is probably what we take
like a simple drink
that is the purpose of our existence
we all die young
it takes a life time we doan have otherwise

our kings are mongrels
our queens are a naked prize
we are tired thieves
and strange natives that really doan belong here
making pride of prey
upon famished lands-

a well kept hard on in the early cold

with very little to say
peer out
see one of the cats crossing the road
there is enough of it all

today suggests to stay up here awhile on the rocks
away from the scampering beasts
under a brass sky whittling the season to a blunt end
only the litany survives
the cock will still crow
broom doan move nah stone

the wind serves a gesture of the coming conditions
I push out a stiff chest
slightly giving in but not so much as to shiver
only going back inside to put on some sleeves
there is a solidarity of sorts
an appreciation for the shrewd iron will
beating existence into a horny hush-

a 16th street memory

I walked out of a frigid gas station bathroom
on the other side of the freeway off ramp
after your girlfriend slid against the wall
and hit the floor
I didn't see you for awhile
and I still haven't

the last I knew, you were a thespian of sorts
working out of the renovated church office
where we used to meet up
insignificant angels taming the stone gargoyles
of inner city roof-tops

knowing our sadness was animated
we lived it out anyway

now I spend my days looking for used books I don't really need
and finding poem in the rust of bones
the blood of soles
and get paid for social work that no one else wants to handle
simply because I've been there with these fuck-ups

I remember
the taste of kissing my arm after loosening the tie-off
I remember how hard it is to care about much else
but that is not true
there isn't anything we can do about it
and this is why
I
think about you
every
so
often-

a long way from retreat

I pulled the car up in front of a row of abandoned houses
on the backside of the city
we waited for our Man
we noticed a few of the habitual others for that time of day
downtrodden
bedraggled
sickened
not as beautiful as we all knew to be

we waited to feel like we owned our soul
we waited to get the fuck out of there

we tried to love each other
as crude as that was
leaning up against one anothers shoulders
with no thought of forever
this should get us through for a bit
hopefully we can pick up on the other side of town later-

the fire is breathing on me

I have enough bones
to hold me up
and take me into what there is of the 11 A.M. sun
I vacation on the streets of Mid-West cities
in all their dinge
during the low degrees
I
can
sit
on a stool at the end of an empty bar room
hang-up the hang-ups
let worry have the woe
as I celebrate the dormant sincerity of the 2 P.M. overcast
staring myself into oblivion
with emphasis on the fire extinguisher
-next to the smoke glazed Natural Light mirror without a frame-
patient to exuberate its cause
and put me out with the rest of this 4 o'clock day
that has jes started
to mend the wounded-

bread and water

the peripheral gone wrong
I am turning around and swinging
until I have circled the block
or the downtown clock
connected the dots into an astringent glare
that I can only make out to be
perversely abstract

and
now
somehow
back to square one

getting up off of my ass
from the sidewalk
and tracing each crack
as if they are the worlds lifeline-

the brave departed and the broken hearted
(the failure of a Lucky Strike)

on the fire-escape
off from the balcony
used to be lovers are quarrelling
in a fluff of air duct steam

they were still dreaming
the season had changed
the harsh now jes cold and rain that dampens half smoked yet lit
cigarettes

the same brand on which she found some other girls lipstick
burnt into the filter
the same brand she found in his pocket of the same jeans he wears
everyday
except that one day last week
the night after the party
when he came home late
(it was more like the next morning when he made his pre-dawn
entrance through the window off from the balcony)
the same one he has carried around ever since he knew this was
going to happen
which is why he made sure the apartment had a fire escape-

the pie is in your mouth

jaw tightens on mashed sugar and cream
keeps saliva form going sour

a sweet beauty
in the sun

I admit I doan try to like everything…
some people are sleeping in the bookstore
some people are staring straight through the books
looking incoherently at a life in front of them

a sweet face
in callous hands

I admit I doan want to like everyone
but girls can be good
with a pinch of salt in their walk
looking their stockings all the way up to a lascivious fit
a modest licking of the cherry on top
if not an all out ravaging…

knowing that you will never kiss empty air
how do you take your coffee
on a fine day for the shrugging of shoulders
and sayonaras'
serving brief attention
to these suggestive matters of mischief
at the pinnacle of our well being-

the constant revolution

we tend to say everyday
as a way to describe
these beaten paths
on these worn out maps
for the way a life elapsing
looks back
with nothing else to ask
this happens
here we see it passing everyday on
easily mistaken
for another sacred instance
not
so
far
gone
a breath may conjure its resistance-

**amongst the relentless love and commotion there is nothing
we need to do about what we don't know**

what is mystery if it is no longer a mystery...
the truth
of the grave
an epitaph on the headstone
a
poem
that answers the riddle
with a sigh
or a snivel
the artillery of war melted down
after it has become another revolution
eyes
that
witness
our own secrets
this is not so horrible
birth
again
given the reliance of reason
indiscriminately
in need of the omnipresent
if not the undisputable devotion to mystery
that keeps us alive-

this time of year I drink on week-day afternoons

"eternity is the state of things at this very moment " Clarice Lispector

the cat had gone into the closet
and didn't come out for days
the wind had calmed down
I went to sleep
under the ceiling there was jes me
but outside there was a moon in the sky

the street-light
of
the world

the color of a candle-lit window
on the other side of town
as you look out at the night-

as always

the effervescent dawn
steadfast
and
begone

there is so much life
with none to be squandered
these arms are not big enough
to hold it all
thus 'Atlas shrugs'
grunts at any measure
tickled by the very girth he juggles upon his shoulder
how often we suggest that this takes courage

the heart jes starting to bulge
from rib and chest
beyond ample youth
arrogant in age, taut of repute
heathen can only nip at ankle
for here
from knee to waste
the sun is thrown back into...-

the tale of a typical Chalant

most of the time I have to adjourn
watch
let these things continue to banter
suspect the backlash to act out a common moronic theme
the surly and its similar
harlots
and
clowns
without their business suits
the day jobs of our whimpering kin

place your suggestions in the box with a name and address
perhaps one might win a spree
the universe in a jar
a mobile to keep above your bed
and gurgle at
with no aura of surprise to deem otherwise
the looking-glass itself an entire sea of entity
salt for the thirsty

walking back from the pilgrimage
thinking the ceremony should have meant more
or at least had a better band of disciples-

not tonight darling (a faded blue sketch)

she had a tattoo on her upper arm
it used to mean everything
now it is the same old nothing she feels
day in day out
that is the destiny, this is her life
she wants a kiss for every hurting heart
that she may commemorate the infliction
how much she yearns
and at jes about every wink of an eye she gets
"fuck you" she says
"fuck you"
not tonight darling
not tonight-

to bunk with an exquisite louse

the afternoon halts mornings calm brilliance
cries out for the wasting of hours
sobering vigor while settling the haze
there is not much but to behave and bellow toward the evening
where the blond irascibility
may be tempered
or seduced from its prosy

hurry from your humble devotions
gather with your fortunes and your meals
tickle the hussy into a nude salute
entrusting the legacy
to rest and awakening-

victory is a stingy beast

how are we to know without swallowing teeth
ah, there is the Gargantua with a large finger in your gullet
strangling all perpetuity from your balls
the cock itself waking you up in the morning
as
soft
as
a buzzard swarms on ragged roadside meat
already picked
reduced to what little there is
of haunch and blood on stone

which is exactly what it took to roll this body out
and ready for the fight
with a bitter fattening lip
there again the imminent wallop
head on
as if I never saw it coming-

down at the sole

there is not enough time
so we might as well pacify its very hindrance
choke out the fiasco
olives or pickles
Heineken or Muscadine
pull the blinds
let the fire in
from now on it is what we used to do
that the wet streets will serenade me by...
the empty house next to the cemetery
the other one next to the overpass
and the one with the green porch
and the ramshackle one right on the train tracks
damn if they weren't all right on the tracks
belligerent as any cackling mockery
and the white one across from the corner store
with the balcony overlooking the ghetto
yes the ghetto

I could cry but I know what it has taken to get me here

and someday, I will throw out the first pitch and wave to the crowd
"He couldn't hit for shit, but by God when he did..."
"He could play the hot corner" and indeed I could
"What ever happened to him? Heard he low-lifed it a bit."
merely a few someday afternoons of slumming it up
"He wrote what?...poem!?, well..." yeah that too

I never did understand this mush
but it feels like the first time you ever get the feeling
baby-

slim to none

everything has its way
do what you will about the fact
the loot is up for grabs
spin
a
wheel
or pick a number
this whole fucking happenstance is rigged
some harbinger has done set the trap
this must be the payback
the crunch under foot
the poke in the eye
the pin the tail on the sorry stooge
well, not so fast
every idiot has something to say before the gun goes off
look for a glimpse of that famous faintest hope
almost always limping from eternity
we
are
all
going to lose blood over whatever is going on here
that's the certain vibe, I get it
but what about the chances to begin with-

with two handfuls of gusto at my leisure

sitting at the desk as if it were a bomb shelter
sparring through some Fante
until the rain came plummeting over the hillside
and I noticed the windows were down on the van

aint that jes life
grab a beer
squeeze the lemon
open the book
rub the hands together
get a good piece of ass on the mind
and THUNDER OF HELL puts its boot at your throat
spreads your own butt clear open
making promises

slap
after
slap

suck back the tears like a man from a last frontier
plunged naked in the ice and wind
watching the sun set
far away
over the sea-

the easiest thing to do

this is not about summer being over
or an emotion or thought about such being so
but it is over
so now
aint it always

here I am a witness to its happening
3 deep
prying open 4
as the monkey collects the curbside coin
the grand parade is loading up and heading out-

we considered everything with the blessings of a saint and a derelict (a dedication of sorts)

the day easily gives in
I piss off the steps and keep nothing hidden

under the burning sails I sharpen my rusted crucifix
the water taste of chlorine and sulfur
I called the atomic hotline
they said there was no threat
it was too calm to imagine such
faith tarnishes

sitting again where we have always been
a corner in this book is bent to mark my place

keep me held in your ranting affection
kissing each tit
sacrificing every lover
we scream, we hit, we are lost to forget
left over for a tomorrow
maybe that is when the small war ends

jes a shutter
open on the window
for the tenderest of air-

no moment of truth is without its deluge

the sun finally broke through the tar in the sky
by the middle of the afternoon
it
has
been
so
long
since we have seen anything other than the palest of light

-I heard
the shadows call out your name-

I am walking across the court-yard
watching people encouraged by such a day
steadying their aim
and setting their fires deeper into the whim-

Mat Gould is walking the ghost back home. This book and its episodes are somewhat a vernacular study. He can not deny his involvement in each charade be it the process of reality or characterization. He is hunkering down and sharpening the spear on the other side of a mountain in Western North Carolina.

Above photo-The Bunkers- by **Gabriel Santerno.** She is from a small town in Northern California. Look for her photography in Badland Days.

cover art: **Tony Max** interprets the world through waking dreams, breathing life into a bizarre fantasy world living within our language, our archetypes and legends He lives in Memphis, Tennessee.
www.hexremoval.blogspot.com

Inset photo by **Abby White**, freelance photographer/designer is hard at work merging all of her desires into one big now.
www.simplebrightmoon.etsy.com

When this book was first published in 2010 I cannot say that we here at Dog On A Chain Press had any idea what we were doing, and I can say as a wise man now that we perhaps still do not. Albeit, we do know why we are doing as we do and it is because of poetry and poets such as this.

This book is our landmark.

"The Fire is Breathing On Me" by Mat Gould represents life as I have known it, honors it by overcoming its brutality, its ignorance, its indifference. Within these pages there is reverence, there is vitality, there is the naked, the wild, the unforeseen and the inevitable heavy breathing that comes along with looking "any beast in the teeth", as it is, as it is going to be, unless something is done about it for oneself…and even then "the loot is up for grabs". So here it is, in a second edition, because we could, because we wanted to, because we did.

Keep a lantern lit,

Beasley Barrenton
Bomb Shelter Maintenance: Dog On A Chain Press

www.ingramcontent.com/pod-product-compliance
Lightning Source LLC
Chambersburg PA
CBHW030312030426
42337CB00012B/684